# HONG KONG

Designed and Produced by

Ted Smart & David Gibbon

MAYFLOWER BOOKS · NEW YORK CITY

# Introduction

IF Sinbad had rubbed Aladdin's lamp and transported a Western city complete on to the Chinese coast he would have ended up with something not unlike Hong Kong. Or so it seems at first impression. From the air, the cubist concrete buildings that rise along the coast of Hong Kong Island and on Kowloon across the bay on the mainland appear to have been deposited, with little regard for the environment, on the ragged coastline which twists and turns like a dragon on a mandarin's coat. A closer look reveals that it is the local environment that has taken over. In the city the Chinese faces outnumber the Western by 99 to 1, in the teeming streets the Chinese signs decorate the shops as if every day was a festival, in the harbors the junks and sampans elbow each other, and at night food markets erupt in car parks and narrow alleys to fill the air with the exotic smell of takeaway foods.

Hong Kong is a place not so much of contrast as of a bewildering variety of different facets. In the total area of 33 square miles which make up the Island and Kowloon there are the business quarter; the old traditional Chinese area of the western district; the nightclubs, topless bars and restaurants of Wanchai on the Island and of Tsim Sha Tsui in Kowloon, and the sampan city at Aberdeen. Up on the Peak are the villas of wealthy residents, and behind Kowloon, in the New Territories that stretch towards the Chinese border, are farms cultivated by peasants in broad-brimmed hats, walled villages and monasteries where life has changed little since Hong Kong was created on the rocky islands where it sits today.

The whole Crown Colony occupies 404 square miles. Its focal point is Victoria Harbor which lies between Hong Kong Island and Kowloon. The harbor, considered one of the world's finest natural ports, was ceded to the British with Hong Kong Island in 1842 and soon became the most important free port in the East with ships from Britain, tea clippers from America, French, Portuguese and Dutch traders trading and discharging their cargoes. Today most travellers arrive by air, landing at Kai Tak Airport, an artificial air strip which juts out into Kowloon Bay.

Hong Kong Island is 29.2 square miles in area and has a population of over a million. It is extremely hilly and dominated by Victoria Peak which rises to 1,808 feet over the Central District, the commercial center of Hong Kong. A tramway ascends to 1,305 feet, from where there is a breath-taking view of harbor and islands that has made travellers place Hong Kong alongside Rio de Janeiro and San Francisco as one of the most spectacular harbors in the world.

Rising out of the Central District are apartment blocks built on terraces carved out of the hillside and, above them on a plateau, is Happy Valley and its race course which is much patronized by the gambling-prone population.

One of the most amazing places on Hong Kong Island's hilly slopes is the Tiger Balm Garden. Its builders, the brothers Aw, were no less remarkable. Aw Boon Haw made a fortune selling an ointment named Tiger Balm which, like the spa waters of nineteenth-century Europe, claimed to cure almost every disease. Whether it did or not, its success led to the founding of a group of businesses and the creation of a garden which with its exotic dragons and oriental buildings amid tropical plants gives pleasure to residents and visitors alike.

The western end of Hong Kong is aptly named West Point and is the oldest quarter of the city. Its winding streets and closely packed houses are almost invisible behind the screen of banners and posters that advertise the presence of thousands of little shops and workshops. There is the atmosphere of a fairground here and the street vendors vie with the shops to attract attention. This is especially true in Cat Street and Ladder Street, though the former is being redeveloped and losing some of its original exuberance. In these streets and in Hollywood Road can be found all kinds of products from ancient Chinese vases, not always genuine, to the bric-a-brac of souvenirs made in imitation ivory. There are all kinds of services offered in the street as well, from fortune-telling to shoe-mending, from hair-dressing to cuisine. A person walking in at one end could come out the other with shoes mended and shined, or with new ones, a new hairstyle, a handmade shirt, manicured hands, a container with takeaway Peking duck, his own horoscope and a jade statue, not to mention a new Japanese camera, quartz watch and just about anything else he could carry or afford.

In Kowloon, across the harbor, the activity is just as frenetic and colorful. Here is the quarter of the big hotels, like the Peninsula, which vies with the Mandarin on Hong Kong Island for the title of the best-known hotel in Hong Kong. This is where the bulk of the tourists who visit Hong Kong will stay and where the shops that cater for them are found in vast numbers. Nathan Road, the principal thoroughfare, was built at the beginning of this century on what was then a relatively undeveloped peninsula, by Sir Matthew Nathan, a former Governor. It was known as Nathan's Folly and even Sir Matthew could not have foreseen the frenetic activity of the scene in the street today. Nathan Road is lined with hotels, shops, department stores, cinemas and arcades and its abundance of signs and banners give it a permanently festive atmosphere.

Kowloon is the fastest-growing part of the Colony and the most industrial; because there is more flat land than on Hong Kong Island, factories and huge apartment blocks to house the working population, nearly a third of them refugees, are going up rapidly.

*In Causeway Bay elegant yachts and smartly fitted launches lie at their spacious Yacht Club moorings.*

Beyond the built-up areas the Hong Kong coastline is very indented and has over 200 islands, the largest of which is Lantau – 'Tai Yue Shan' in Chinese which means 'Big Island Mountain'.

Lantau is 55 square miles in area but has only 20,000 inhabitants, most of whom live in the ferry and fishing port of Tai O on the northwest coast. It is an attractive town, with the wooden houses of fishermen built on stilts in the main creek. Fish are found around the island, but the fierceness of the competition from other fishermen in the Hong Kong area drives the more intrepid men out to sea to try their luck in deeper waters. While the men fish, the women stay at home and help in other local industries such as the making of shrimp paste and the processing of salt fish.

The island is an attractive place to escape to from the bustle of Kowloon and Hong Kong Island and is a favorite place for walkers, despite the abundance of snakes, none of which are, however, poisonous. The main ferry ports, besides Tai O, are Tung Chung further west where there is the ruin of an old fort, and Mui Wo in the southeast. Mui Wo or Silvermine Bay is a good place from which to set off for the beaches that lie along the coast and for the Po Lin Monastery high up in the center of the island which has Hong Kong's only tea plantation. Nearer the coast at Mui Wo is another monastery, where Trappist monks who were driven out of Peking in 1948, have since lived.

To the south of Lantau lies Cheung Chau Island, a small rocky island which becomes the center of attention in May when the Bun Festival takes place on it. The high point of this colorful event culminates with the attempted ascent of three huge pyramids of buns by those taking part.

The main land surface of Hong Kong is not provided by islands but by the 370 square miles of the New Territories. This land, leased from the Chinese in 1898 for 99 years, has been the granary of Hong Kong and the source of its water supply. Every inch of the low-lying land is cultivated and along the lower slopes the abstract patterns of terraced fields follow the contours of the hills. Even in the higher plateaus of the hills, the earth lying between the bare rocks is carefully planted and cared for.

Down in the valleys the paddyfields mirror the sky in their water and the peasants who work in them in their broad-brimmed hats look like an ancient Chinese painting.

This picture reflects the essential nature of the Territories and people who live there more than words can express. Here are the patient, persevering people whose way of life and fundamental beliefs have changed little since the time when Hong Kong was a relatively uninhabited and treeless land. Many of them still live in the fortified villages huddled tightly inside their walls and they do not welcome strangers, although this attitude is changing under the influence of the cosmopolitan life of the city of Kowloon which rises at the southern end of the peninsula.

To ease the pressure of housing in the urban areas of Kowloon and Hong Kong, three new cities are being built in the Territories. These will house a million of the one and a half million people for whom accommodation has to be found in the next ten years. Even with the new towns, there will still be plenty of space in the New Territories, in the two huge curving bays of Port Shelter and Rocky Harbor to the east and the vast indentation which sweeps into the island as far as the railway which runs north and south from Kowloon to Lo Wu at the Chinese border.

But the destiny of all Hong Kong rests on the urban areas of Kowloon and Victoria, the city on Hong Kong Island which is usually referred to as Hong Kong. It is here that the bulk of the four and a half million population live and work in a tightly packed area bordering Victoria Harbor.

This mass of humanity, 99 per cent of it Chinese, supported by the resources and inventiveness of Western industrial society, is what Hong Kong is all about. Here capital and labor have reacted with the same dynamic force that produced industrial Europe over a hundred years ago and the United States of America even more recently.

Maintaining law and order and dispensing justice over this seething cauldron is the Governor, appointed by the British Government of Her Majesty Queen Elizabeth II. The Governor administers the Colony with an Executive Council and a Legislative Council and Justice is based on English Common Law and the rules of equity.

The meteoric growth of population over the past thirty years has not made things easy. Since 1948, when refugees from mainland China started to arrive, the population has increased from 1.8 million to 4.6 million.

When the refugees first began pouring in, the Colony lived on trade with China and government revenue was insufficient to cope with the demands of hundreds of thousands of unemployed and homeless people from the mainland. However, with the poor refugees there also came enterprising businessmen who were no longer persona grata in the People's Republic; they, with the help of Western capital and Western business methods, brought about the economic miracle of Hong Kong.

The miracle has not been unblemished. At first, the labor force had to house itself and conditions were appalling, with the government unable or unwilling to do anything about it. Eventually a more enlightened administration took on the responsibility for a social welfare program which included the development of social security, programs of community services, welfare for individuals and families, and care for the physically disabled and the old. A vast rehousing program was begun and today more than two million people live in government-owned or sponsored houses and apartments.

The struggle to survive and to improve standards of life is unending, and despite the tenfold increase in revenue since the 1960s Hong Kong cannot stay still. The expectations of the population, competition from nearby countries like South Korea and Singapore, and the lack of growth in the world economy are all potential dangers to the Hong Kong community. So Hong Kong looks continually for new industrial development and new markets.

To make communications with the rest of the world easier, Hong Kong has built an airport into Kowloon Bay. This airstrip is used by thirty of the world's airlines providing more than 900 scheduled passenger services to and from Hong Kong each week, as well as cargo flights that carry the products of Hong Kong manufacture all over the world.

Hong Kong's principal market is the USA, followed by West Germany and Great Britain; principal imports, many of them foodstuffs and raw materials to feed the people and the factories, come from Japan and China. Apart from manufacturing and commerce, Hong Kong lives off a growing tourist trade. In 1977, over one and a half million visitors enjoyed the attractions of the Crown Colony. The majority, about 500,000, were Japanese and 250,000 were from North America, with Britain contributing some 70,000.

This influx of visitors has had a significant effect on the life of Hong Kong and on the amenities to be found in the urban centers of Hong Kong and Kowloon. Like most tourists, the visitor to Hong Kong looks for good accommodation, restaurants, places of entertainment and cheap shopping; Hong Kong has provided these with the same verve and dedication that it expends on trade.

The tourist is catered for equally well on Hong Kong Island and in mainland Kowloon, though the latter has an edge over the Island in the number of its hotels, because the flatter land of the peninsula gives more room for expansion and building. Around the great hotels are the densest shopping areas in the world: so many shops crammed together in streets and specially-built arcades that the visitor wonders how they can all make a living.

Despite the evident struggle for survival, the Hong Kong shopkeeper is restrained in his salesmanship, and no one is subjected to the touting for business that is a disagreeable feature of other great tourist centers. The shops stock every imaginable item and no doubt, if requested to, could produce even the unimaginable for a customer. Many of the goods for sale are from the Chinese mainland, for despite the many factors that might seem to weigh against the existence of a capitalist enclave on the flanks of a great Communist power, Hong Kong has a continuing relationship with the People's Republic. The existence of the Bank of China in its great building in the Central District of Hong Kong is a sign that some things are stronger than mere politics.

Most visitors are not bothered by the politics of the situation nor even with the morality of it, however, nor is the average resident of Hong Kong. As in most parts of the world, the ordinary people are concerned with getting on with their lives and making ends meet; despite its affluence, this is no easy matter in over-crowded Hong Kong.

In this densely populated free port it is inevitable that the crime rate should be high, a problem aggravated in Hong Kong by the high rate of hard drug addiction coupled with the tourists' demands in the world of entertainment. In recent years, the growth of topless bars, massage parlors and other esoteric titillations has increased markedly, as it has in other tourists' Edens.

Hong Kong has plenty of more innocent entertainments of course. There are over 3,000 restaurants serving the most delectable food in the most courteous manner; there are superb beaches without, as in other tourist areas, thousands upon thousands of deck chairs lined along the sand; there are beautiful walks, there are museums, theaters, concert halls: everything, in fact, that assures the continuing success of Hong Kong as a tourist as well as a business center.

The future for Hong Kong, however, has a question mark hanging over the year 1997, when the lease of the New Territories from China expires. At this time Hong Kong Island, which was ceded to Britain in perpetuity, will be isolated, retaining none of the land from which it now draws much of its food, water and other essentials. Can it survive alone? Will the Peking Government claim back the land that belongs to it? No one knows the answers to these questions. The new, warm relationship between China and Britain and the undoubted value that Hong Kong has had as a gateway between China and the West, even in the most difficult years of ideological conflict, have led some people to believe that Hong Kong will continue on its course as the most successful trading and tourist center in Asia. But no one really knows. As for the people of Hong Kong, they are pragmatists, taking things as they come and contributing to them all the energy, and imagination that has built up one of the most remarkable cities in the world.

Overleaf: *Along the waterfront, skyscrapers glow in the evening light beneath the distinctive rise of Victoria Peak.*

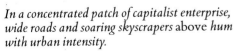

*In a concentrated patch of capitalist enterprise, wide roads and soaring skyscrapers above hum with urban intensity.*

*Between the Hong Kong Club and the Courts of Justice far left stands the cenotaph.*

*In the late, hot summer, mighty typhoons roar across the China Sea, creating havoc, and the fragile junks and sampans resort to refuges such as the Causeway Bay Typhoon Shelter left.*

*The race course at Happy Valley above, center and below right opens for the racing season between October and May.*

*Dazzling lights overleaf illuminate a myriad of shops, restaurants, offices and apartment blocks.*

Hong Kong's bustling street markets have all the atmosphere and excitement of the Orient. Here a confusion of rickshaws and shoppers jostle their way between a wide variety of colorful stalls, laden with every kind of fruit and vegetable as well as livestock and cooked delicacies. Here also a multitude of services, ranging from fortune-telling to shoe-mending, are offered to the passer-by.

The Star Ferry overleaf has been carrying passengers across the harbor since 1880 when the steam launches of Dorabjee Nowrojee first initiated the service.

# A Day In The Life of Hong Kong

EARLY rising is the rule in Hong Kong and soon after sunrise the streets are full of people hurrying to work. They come from the vast new apartment blocks, from the shanties made of flattened tin cans and bamboo down in the valleys, from the sampans in the harbors, and from the houses that crowd against each other in the city streets. This tide of humanity walks, rides bicycles or hangs determinedly onto the overcrowded trams to get to work.

Down Nathan Road, the red London-style double-decker buses line up with cars and taxis, just as if they were in their native London, and at the wharves of both Kowloon and Hong Kong Central District the crowds wait to board the Star ferries.

Those who have to cross the harbor to get to work are the lucky ones, for their day starts with a panoramic view that lifts the spirits of all but the sleepiest. As the ferry plows its way across the calm waters the eye takes in the great complex of buildings lining the shore, and above them on the island side the steeply sloping outline of the Peak silhouetted against the morning light. On the Kowloon side the nine hills which separate the city from the New Territories form a backcloth to the buildings; beyond rise the hills of China.

Motorists miss the view, for they cross the harbor through the tunnel. Soon, the bulk of commuters will miss it also, for they will be confined to the tunnel or the subway which is now in the process of construction. For most workers, concerned only with the speed with which they can get to work, perhaps the early morning view will not be missed as much as a romantic outsider likes to think, especially during the typhoon season from May to October when a ride across the harbor can lack the charm it displays during the fine winter months.

With the rush hour comes activity at all the streetside stalls. Old ladies set up their news-stands, no more than a table on which the papers and magazines pinned together with clothes-pins cascade to the pavement; food stalls offer hot drinks and snacks; street markets set out their wares; the professional scribes, who earn their living by writing letters for the illiterate, set up their tables; the sign writers hang out their good luck scrolls along the walls.

For most of the workers the factory is no more than a room in which they will spend the day cutting and sewing garments, carving intricate *objets d'art* out of ivory, assembling electronic equipment, ironing, cooking, washing and providing the thousands of services which the busy city requires. Others will work in banks and business houses or in the larger textile mills, shipbuilding yards, or domestic appliance factories. Those who work for the larger organizations have the benefits of good, well-organized environments and free medical care, as well as subsidized housing; the others have a range of conditions varying from an overcrowded slum of Dickensian squalor to the bright, modern but compact surroundings of a small but successful individual business.

In the early morning the markets are a scene of immense activity as the buyers from restaurants, as well as private citizens, haggle over the price of produce. In the market stalls the women prepare the vegetables and fruit for sale, chop up sugar cane into short sticks, select the live fish from tanks of water for prospective customers, chop up meat, and are always ready to bring off a quick sale when the opportunity presents itself.

Midday is signalled by the firing of a gun in the grounds of Jardine Matheson, the company which traces its beginnings to the two hardy Scots who established their business during the nineteenth century. The rush hour now begins again for those who work near enough to their homes to snatch a short break with their families. Most people adopt the custom of Western cities and crowd the snack bars or street-side foodstalls. Here one may see rows of men not sitting but crouching on the benches, bowl in one hand and chop sticks in the other and carrying on animated conversations. The well-to-do businessmen meet at restaurants and, later on in the afternoon, at tea places, where the long and subtle negotiations required to bring a deal to a conclusion are carried out.

When not hard at work the Hong Kong people enjoy their leisure in both Chinese and Western styles. Soccer is followed with as much enthusiasm as elsewhere in the world and Hong Kong teams play against opponents from as far away as South America and Africa. Basketball is another imported game that has many followers and there are plenty of courts provided by the government in community centers and public parks. The universal game, enjoyed by people of all ages, is mah-jong. This is played with domino-size tiles bearing Chinese characters and con-sists of a variety of games similar to Western card games. As with most card games, mah-jong lends itself to gambling and at any time of day or night a visitor may come across a group of figures bent over a table with intense concentration as the tiles are moved rapidly with a crisp clicking sound and the money changes hands even more quickly. On warm summer evenings one of the favorite places for a quiet un-disturbed game of mah-jong is a sampan afloat in the harbor.

The setting of the sun does not mark the end of the working day for the Hong Kong people but it is the starting point of the homeward rush hour and the signal that nightlife is about to begin. The night street vendors appear, pushing their carts laden with food, the cafés and restaurants and nightclubs switch on their neon signs and the busy street life of Hong Kong shifts gear for the long, uphill climb towards another dawn.

*At the water's edge, a small girl left shelters from the glare of the sun, beneath a colorful parasol.*

Although rising wages for workers and plentiful opportunities for gifted entrepreneurs are helping to bridge the gap between the few very rich and the millions of poor, for many Hong Kong residents, the basic necessities of life: rice, water and a little territory to call home, are still difficult to come by. Moored alongside sleek pleasure cruisers, an entanglement of congested sampans creates a floating world in which entire families live, breed and die.

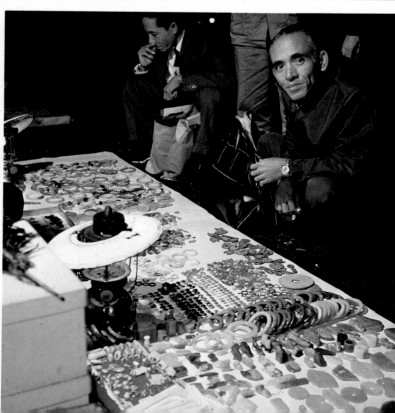

The Colony's place among the world leaders in the output of toys like those displayed on the pavement above, provides strong evidence of its manufacturing and mercantile wizardry. Hong Kong's energy and its spirit of enterprise must, however, frequently find an outlet in conditions that would be inconceivable to the Westerner, whether it be in a small corner of one of the many crowded streets or on its equally congested waters left, above right and right.

Chinese water babies far left huddle in their floating home in the chill of a winter's night.

Overleaf: Taken from Peak Tower on Victoria Peak…a breathtaking view of the 'Fragrant Harbor'. In the distance the airport runway reaches out into the vivid blue waters.

Hong Kong is a gourmet's paradise, where an almost obsessive preoccupation with food gives rise to envious comments that the inhabitants live to eat. Among the Chinese expressions of greeting is the polite inquiry: 'Have you eaten?' Dating back to days of extreme poverty, the expression shows a tender regard for the stomach, which has not changed through the centuries. On the site of a daytime car park, the 'Poor Man's Night Club' on these pages and overleaf provides open stalls laden with cooked delicacies of all kinds.

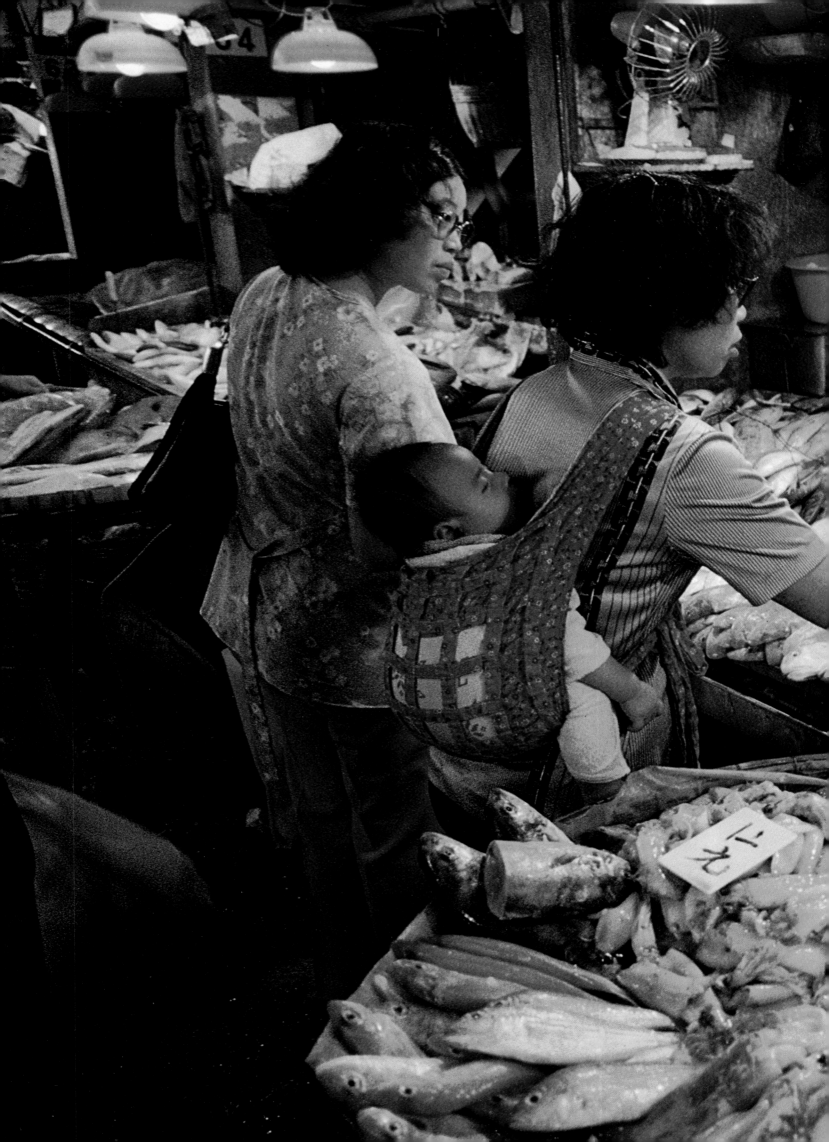

# The Laughing Dragon

THERE are good grounds for claiming that Hong Kong is the most festive place on earth. Rio has its Carnival, Nice its Battle of Flowers and New Orleans its Mardi Gras, but what other city has streets that appear to be eternally bedecked for a celebration? Besides, in Hong Kong the festivals are not once a year but are celebrated frequently, marking the high points of the lunar calendar.

The festivals are not events organized for the tourist but are real and traditional parts of life for Chinese people, reflecting deeply-felt beliefs about natural phenomena, rhythms of the seasons and social relationships.

The most important of these events that mark the progress of the year is the New Year Festival. This, with its preparatory period, lasts several days. The Chinese New Year begins on the twentieth day of the Twelfth Moon and is essentially a time for renovation and looking forward, a period for reaffirmation of beliefs and identification with those who form part of one's environment. The Hong Kong people start the New Year with a vigorous spring cleaning of their houses, and give each other flowers, especially peach blossoms which traditionally frighten away demons, thereby leaving the field clear for the good things of life. Evil spirits are also frightened away by the traditional Chinese method of lighting firecrackers.

During this period, the streets of Hong Kong are filled with people hurrying to visit relatives or, in the early part of the festival, going to shrines to pay respect to their ancestors. In the early days there is also a distribution of packets of money to aged or unmarried relatives and to children. In this way the continuity of life and the responsibility of family members for each other are affirmed.

As the festival progresses, special days are devoted to different objectives. There is a day for firing employees in a polite and unobtrusive manner by simply referring to their past work but not mentioning the future, and there is a day devoted to the god of the kitchen; this is also a day for married daughters to visit their parents.

The day dedicated to the god of wealth not unnaturally demands that everyone should get up early. On Lantern Day, paper lanterns with words such as Fortune, Dignity, or Birth written on them are lit and hung in the temples; one might call these prayer lanterns as they evidently express the hidden wishes of those who hang them.

There is a great deal of eating and drinking, with friends and relatives gathered together, and the ubiquitous Chinese dragon with the face of a startled Pekingese, a traditional part of any street procession, winds its way among the festivities with its red mane waving and its human feet dancing along the roadway.

Another important festival is dedicated to Nam Hai Hsing, the god who is reputed to have taught the Chinese the use of fire. The god, who has a fearsome face and wears an elaborate headdress, receives obeisances and offers of food from the people. A more gentle festival reflecting the Chinese care for nature, is the Festival of the Birthday of Flowers which is appropriately on the fifteenth day of the Second Moon in springtime.

Many of the festivals are fairly private affairs concerning only the celebrants and the god or goddess who represents the quality or seasonal event which is being acknowledged. The Festival of the Goddess of Mercy, Kuan Yin, for example, consists of visits to the temples and the presentation of gifts of cakes to her. The cakes are usually consumed after a religious ceremony.

Other festivals are more public and become colorful spectacles in which everyone joins. Of these, one of the most spectacular is the Dragon Boat Festival which is held on the fifth day of the Fifth Moon. According to legend, the poet Chu Yuan, concerned about the decadence of government, drowned himself in protest against the injustice and corruption of those in power. On discovering his self-sacrifice the people launched their boats and tried to recover his body while throwing rice cakes into the river to distract the sharks. The evocation of this event has been carried out in China since time immemorial. In Hong Kong, it takes places in the harbor where dragon boats compete with each other every year for pennants and prizes. The scene is akin to that of a great regatta and there is color and noise and laughter throughout the day.

Another very popular and unusual festival is the Bun Festival, held on Cheung Chau Island for four days from the eighth day of the Fourth Moon. On the waterfront, three huge cones of buns are erected under scaffolding covered with colorful banners. The first day of the festival is devoted to eating vegetarian meals, burning paper clothes for ghosts in need of raiment, and lighting incense candles. The celebrations on the third day reach a climax with the ascent of the bun cones. At a given signal, all those participating begin to ascend the cones, collecting as many buns as they can in sacks attached to their waists. The competition is fierce, for there is status to be gained as well as the buns which are later sold to spectators unable or unwilling to take part. Parades, music, fireworks and all the other accouterments of a grand-style celebration accompany the Bun Festival.

One festival has declined in popularity in the Chinese calendar of events, perhaps because it has gradually been superseded by the kind of Christmas that is rapidly becoming universal. This is the Festival of the Winter Solstice on December 22, which was an important date for farmers in the Chinese calendar. In an industrial community such as Hong Kong, now overlaid with Western customs and culture, it might be expected that other festivals would also have suffered an eclipse but this is not so, for the Chinese ways of life and beliefs remain as strong and colorful as ever.

*Sun sets over the quietening harbor's ships and the evening ferry with its cargo of weary commuters returning home.*

Many of Hong Kong's buildings, like the majestically domed Supreme Court *left*, date back to the old colonial days.

*The Cross Harbor Tunnel above right, opened in August 1972, is believed to be the largest submersed tube tunnel in the world.*

*A funicular cable car above climbs to a height of 1,305 ft. above sea level to the exotic and famous Tiger Balm Gardens on Victoria Peak right and below right. In gardens which reflect the oriental passion for precision in their landscaping, fascinating grottoes and pavilions display statues from Chinese mythology.*

*Below: an exquisite example of hand-carved ivory.*

*The dynamic atmosphere of Hong Kong's concrete congestion overleaf presents an unforgettable panorama.*

The demands of the pantheon of Chinese gods and goddesses are numerous; they must be respected, revered, flattered and occasionally entertained with extravagant spectacles. So, joss sticks are burned, masks are donned and lions and dragons are paraded through the streets amidst a carcophony of music and drums to encourage them to look with favor on their human subjects.

The modernity of Hong Kong is exemplified by its numerous street signs overleaf.

# Behind The Mask

WESTERNERS have long harbored a belief that the Chinese are inscrutable, and therefore impossible to understand or to reach an understanding with. Was this an imperialist myth designed to relieve the Westerner from responsibility for his failure to come to terms with the Chinese Empire? Or was it and is it a fact?

In Hong Kong, where Chinese and Westerner live and work closely together, there is an opportunity to study the encounter of the two cultures and to draw some conclusions about the truth or falsehood of this popular belief.

At first sight, the Chinese appear no more difficult to understand than the Westerner who inhabits the Colony. Most dress in Western style, they express themselves freely with much gesture and emotive expression, they work hard, they are attentive and efficient – in fact, to many visiting Western businessmen faced with an argumentative labor force back home, the Chinese appear to be the very epitome of the kind of Englishman who built the Empire.

But surfaces often simply reflect the person looking at them and conceal what goes on underneath. To some extent, this is so in Hong Kong. Despite the appearance that they have embraced Western styles of life, the Hong Kong Chinese are deeply attached to their own traditions and beliefs. One need not go far to discover the reason why: the majority of the Chinese in the Colony are emigrants from the mainland. They left their homes, their farms and their businesses in towns and villages where they and their fathers before them had lived for generations, and settled in an entirely new land governed by foreigners whom they had always regarded with suspicion and distrust. They therefore cling to the roots which give them stability and security, and the medium through which these roots are confirmed is the family.

Strangely enough this situation is reflected in the lives of the Westerners who live and work in Hong Kong. They too are in a sense a transient community, either on contract to a company that has business there or working for the government, and all of them are aware that Hong Kong as they know it might be facing extinction in 1997, the year that the lease on the New Territories expires. So they, too, cling to old traditions, many of which are no longer in tune with the contemporary world of international trade and politics.

Such a tenuous state of affairs has hardly been conducive to the concept of working for a future together. But recent events are helping to change that. With the new outward-looking policy of the People's Republic and its increasing trade and cultural ties with Western countries, a new era has begun which cannot but affect deeply the Chinese people who form the majority of Hong Kong's population.

Of the two cultures, it is the Chinese one that is likely to be most affected by closer contact between China and the West. The reason for this is that the Chinese way of life is based on deeply-held philosophical beliefs, which have not, until now, been exposed to the materialistic and iconoclastic ways of Western thought. The basis of all Chinese life is the family, and this includes parents, children, grandparents, uncles, aunts – in fact, all relatives by blood or marriage. The family is a clan, with all members showing respect for their seniors and acknowledging the oldest male as the head. Ethics, morality and even religion are influenced by the family unit and the actions of one member of the group reflect on the whole. In these circumstances, the individual action which is the rule in Western society does not occur and most major decisions are those with which the family as a whole concurs.

In Hong Kong, the effect of Western life on the clan system is already evident and Chinese society is going through a change analogous to that which overtook Western communities at the end of the nineteenth and beginning of the twentieth centuries. Formal marriages have become the exception rather than the rule and young Hong Kong Chinese are leaving their family groups to travel and work all over the world. The impact of Western culture is strongest in the battle for sexual equality, and in Hong Kong women are able to become teachers, scientists or doctors, and often work beside men in factories and offices.

It is difficult to visualize what the final effect of Western culture will be on people whose traditions go back thousands of years. The waning of the self-confidence that filled the West until World War II may diminish the impact, and the spread of ideas from every part of the world may dilute it. In any case, Western ideas do not fall into a vacuum in Hong Kong as they once did in the colonial era. The people of Hong Kong are aware of events in the rest of the world and of other ideologies and philosophies.

Perhaps one of the strengths of the Chinese way of life is that its religious basis is founded on philosophical ideas and not on exclusive doctrines. Confucius was not divine – he was a thinker who propounded certain ideas for the achievement of an ideal society. Confucius taught the importance of family as a unit of society and similarly Taoism emphasizes the importance of maintaining a close bond with nature; later Buddhism arrived with its ideas of salvation through self-sacrifice.

Whatever, happens, destiny has chosen Hong Kong as the spearhead of the new encounter between East and West, and Hong Kong represents the melting-pot experience which will soon be undergone by the Chinese people as a whole.

*Beneath giant, suspended coils of incense, joss sticks burn before the ornate altar of the Man Mo Temple, to honor the two deities: Man Cheong, the civil god and Kwan Kung, the martial god.*

There are some 600 Chinese temples in Hong Kong, rich in treasures such as the gilded figure above. Of these, half are Buddhist and about 200 Taoist. The Man Mo Temple above left is a place of Taoist worship, built in 1842, around the time when Hong Kong itself was founded.

The Ching Chung Koon (Long Life Temple) left and below far left is another Taoist temple, set in magnificent gardens containing a valuable collection of 'pun joy' or miniature trees below left.

Above right: a Taoist official presides over professional mourners at the funeral of a woman, whose photograph is displayed on the altar.

One of the best known Buddhist temples is the Po Lin (Precious Lotus) right, of which the inner sanctuary is guarded by carved wooden lions.
The Seal-keeper and Thousand-Li Eye below stand before the goddess, Tin Hau in a temple dedicated to the Taoist Queen of Heaven.

The ornate 'pai lau' above forms an imposing entrance to the Ching Chung temple.

Behind the main altar in the temple of 10,000 Buddhas left and right rows of gilded images, each one different in posture or gesture, are said to represent actual Buddhas, former humans who achieved enlightenment and were rewarded with salvation.

The body of Yuet Kai below, the monk who founded this unique temple, has been preserved in gold.

Hong Kong's harbor is pictured by night overleaf.

*The hazy silhouettes of ships and boats left
drift in the most spectacular seascapes.*

*A rickshaw coolie above awaits a fare. Like
the sedan-chair, rickshaws are fast becoming
an obsolete form of transport.*

*At night the fountains outside the Hotel
Peninsula above right are suffused with
golden light and in the distance the
illuminations of the Ocean Terminal right
glimmer across the water.*

*Birds in elegant cages below are particularly
favored as pets by the older generation
Chinese.*

*In the Riverside Restaurant, Food Street
below right, a mouthwatering display of
Chinese food includes the famous Peking
duck, hot melon soup and noodles made not by
machine but by exceptionally deft hands.*

51

# The Sleepless City

HONG KONG boasts that life goes on twenty-four hours a day in its twin cities of Kowloon and Victoria. Even before the workers have finished their ten-hour daily stint the nightlife has begun – if, indeed, it can be called nightlife, for much of the entertainment that comes under that heading never stops. Bars, strip joints and massage parlors are open in the daytime as well as at night. But nightfall does produce a change in atmosphere and tempo, as millions bent on pleasure prepare for the night show of the Hong Kong spectacle.

The first item in the show is, for many people, the most memorable of all. It is the age-old drama of the sun setting over one of the most beautiful harbors in the world. The magic of the sun sinking under a blazing sky, with the horizon merging into it, to reappear phoenix-like in a blaze of neon, is breathtaking. At this time of day, the connoisseur takes the Peak tramway and views the scene from a vantage point above Hong Kong, looking across the harbor to Kowloon and the mountains of China beyond.

Down below, the restaurants are receiving the first diners; in the dance halls the women begin their nightly wait for customers, the bars fill with sailors, and the night excursions take off from the hotels in buses crowded with Japanese, British, American and other visitors from all over the world. For most of them, the excursions will be fairly innocuous, following regular patterns over routes designed to show 'typical' Hong Kong scenes without offending the sensibilities of more easily shocked visitors. But the tourist route only skims the surface of the Hong Kong night. Once the tourists get out of their buses, they find that Hong Kong night life provides entertainment for all levels of budget, taste and proclivity.

At the calmer, more urbane end of the spectrum there are the big hotels with their comfortable bars and international-style restaurants at which prices are in the top range and service is provided by formally attired waiters, or by waitresses elegantly dressed in silk cheong sams. Restrained sophistication is the keynote there and in the floorshows at the hotel nightclubs, where international stars appear backed by bevies of beautiful girls in spectacular costumes.

Hong Kong's large well-appointed ballrooms provide a meeting place of a different kind. Here one can meet friends, entertain business acquaintances and dance with the hostesses for a moderate fee. This usually covers a twenty-minute period, and a controller ensures that if the time is exceeded it is paid for. If the customer wants to take the girl out, he must pay a 'ransom' fee which varies according to the amount of time left between the request for her company and the closing of the ballroom.

Bars are the most prolific of all Hong Kong's nightspots, and their neon signs are superimposed on each other in a spectacular kaleidoscope of garish colors. Girls abound, as the signs take pains to point out, and customers rarely find themselves alone for long. The price of female company is two drinks, one real and the other a mock whisky or champagne for the girl. Overseeing the whole operation is a Chinese lady 'Mama–san', a kind of 'Madame' who makes sure that profit and pleasure are satisfactorily balanced. In recent years more and more bars have become topless by popular demand.

A more sophisticated version of the topless bar is the hostess bar, which is specially popular with the Japanese who make up the majority of Hong Kong tourists today. At the hostess bar, the visitor pays a fee for the company of the hostess and drinks are more expensive than at an ordinary bar.

Small hotels, where rooms may be hired by the hour, are an essential part of the night scene. So, too, is the continual touting in the streets for pornographic literature, as well as all the other services associated with nighttime pleasure.

Not all pleasures are sexual, however, and the nightworld has many other fascinating aspects. There are the street markets for example, the most noteworthy of which is the one known as the Poor Man's Nightclub. This is set up every evening near the Macao ferry terminal and becomes a veritable fairground, with stalls selling every conceivable type of merchandise and the air filled with the smell of frying fish and roasting meat. Included among the crowds are the wandering entertainers, acrobats, jugglers, fortune tellers and conjurers who give the name of nightclub to the market.

For gambling on a big scale, however, one has to go to the old Portuguese port of Macao, 45 minutes away by hydrofoil on the mainland. This is the Las Vegas of the East, with every form of gambling available, from the sophisticated and stylish Casino de Lisboa to slot machines in the bars or the Chinese game of fan tan, in which one guesses at the number of beans in a jar.

Remembering that night is for romance, Hong Kong can also provide one of the world's most exciting evenings out for lovers: a night ride on a sampan. This is the Chinese equivalent of a trip on a Venetian gondola. But there is a difference, for on the sampan one can also eat the food sold by the kitchen sampans that rove about the bay dispensing snacks and cooked meals. In their floating bower under cover of a reed canopy, lovers can enjoy not only each other's company but the magical spectacle of Hong Kong at night.

*With meticulous care, shoppers* left *select the best buys from the vast range of fruit and vegetables that confronts them.*

*Overleaf: The Ocean Terminal and Ocean Center buildings and the tower of the old railway station overlook the almost motionless water of the harbor.*

In the neon jungle of Hong Kong's congested streets, bi-lingual signs advertise everything from massage parlors to the world's finest materials, especially silk. The skilled Chinese tailors are renowned for supplying clothes, made-to-measure in just a few hours.

Against the night sky overleaf, the commercial giants continue to compete, for the selling never really stops.

裕華

CHINESE PRODUCTS

新世界大廈
THE WORLD DRUG

Even before the workers have finished their ten-hour stint, the nightlife has begun. Nightfall produces a change in atmosphere and tempo, as millions bent on pleasure prepare for the night show of the Hong Kong spectacle in clubs like the Bottoms Up or the Mikado.

After the night-time festivities, daylight brings reality to Hong Kong's crowded streets overleaf.

Inside the Hotel Miramar, Kowloon, dinner is served to the accompaniment of nightly performances of a now famous Chinese floor show, including acrobatic, operatic and song and dance acts, which have long been popular with the tourists.

Overleaf: *Nathan Road, Kowloon, by night. Because of the proximity of Kaitak Airport, the neon lights never flash.*

# Frogs and Snails and Puppy Dogs' Tails

OST of the ingredients of which little boys and girls are supposed to be made, according to the old nursery rhyme, are available in Hong Kong's encyclopedic menus, with more besides, and all put together with a care that only dedicated cooks give to their food. For those who like the taste of the exotic, the Chinese do wonders with snakes, monkeys and cats, though dogs are now illegal fare.

If the Hong Kong chefs are superb, they have to be, with competition from something like 3,000 restaurants – large, small, specializing in every kind of food from all over the world, and giving impeccable service. Most restaurants are in the Hong Kong and Kowloon areas, but there are many others scattered along the coast.

As in most things Chinese, the preparation of food includes a sprinkling of philosophy, as well as exotic spices, and the principles of yin and yang, the interplaying forces which when balanced correctly bring harmony to life, provide the basis of much gastronomic invention. Many of the ingredients have homeopathic powers and are added to the food to promote good health and general well-being.

The glow of satisfaction arising from a good meal is further enhanced in Hong Kong by the quality of attention that the diner receives. The menus are so vast that, to paraphrase Doctor Johnson's comments on London, a man who gets tired of Hong Kong food must be tired of eating. The hot towels brought at the beginning and end of the meal are as refreshing as the tea that is served liberally throughout the meal.

The most widespread style of food, not surprisingly considering the proximity and historic connections of the city with the colony, is that of Canton. This cuisine, with its sweet-sour, bland-sharp contrasts, is what the majority of people think of as Chinese food, especially in dishes such as sweet and sour pork and in the Dim Sum menu which, though generally eaten throughout China, is particularly varied in Cantonese cooking. Dim Sum appeals to the eye as much as to the taste; when the pagodas of little straw baskets appear, each holding a delicately flavoured morsel such as a prawn dumpling, or rice in lotus leaf, or fluffy pork buns, there is all the fun of opening the baskets as well as eating their contents.

Everyone has heard of thousand-year-old eggs. In Western countries they have long been a gastronomic joke as a result of ignorance concerning the true nature of this Cantonese delicacy. Thousand-year-old eggs are eggs preserved in earth and ashes for a few months, so that they acquire the look of archeological specimens. Their taste is far removed from the dusty odor of museums and, with young pickled ginger as an accompaniment, they are among the great taste delights of the world.

Rivaling Canton's culinary fame is that of Peking, whose cuisine grew out of a need to satisfy the demands of Emperors, some of whom would sit down to meals of over one hundred dishes. Peking duck comes immediately to mind as a fine example of the Peking style. When eaten in the proper way, the crispy duck flesh wrapped in a paper-thin pancake with a sliver of spring onion or cucumber and a dollop of plum sauce, it does indeed seem food fit for an imperial palate. There are other no less spectacular dishes for the connoisseur of exotic food, such as Beggars chicken, baked in ashes and wrapped in lotus leaves, or the Peking barbecue, or Bear's paws.

Among the out-of-town places for food, Aberdeen, whose floating restaurants are lit up like amusement parks at night, and are anchored among the great town of sampans in the bay, is well worth a visit. Here, diners can enjoy the world's most extraordinary collection of seafood, most of it alive in tanks attached to the restaurant until called in to the frying pan or grill.

Inimitable parts of Hong Kong's eating life are the many open-air eating markets that spring up in the evening in any available open space. The most famous of these is the so-called 'Poor Man's Nightclub' near the Macao ferry terminal in Hong Kong. Here, hundreds upon hundreds of stalls fill the night air with the smell of their cooking; alongside, the largest open-air market in Hong Kong provides entertainment of a different kind.

In Hong Kong it is even possible to take a meal on a sampan – if one has the stomach for the up-and-down motion. Most sampans are found in sheltered areas such as Causeway Bay and Yaumati, which are recognized shelter from the winds of the typhoon season.

Though most visitors to Hong Kong are prepared for the exotic delicacy and variety of the food, they are often taken aback by the down-to-earth decor of most restaurants. Other than those designed for the tourist, who may like to find himself in the familiar ambience of English pubs, Austrian Stuberls, Italian trattorias or other 'typical' settings, Chinese restaurants are simply a room in which to eat, for the local residents do not demand elaborate decors and tables are often large, rather than intimately small, to accommodate family parties.

Like many other nations with a strong sense of the importance of family life, the Hong Kong Chinese like to get together with relatives and friends. Since many of them live in cramped surroundings, with limited cooking facilities and living room space, the restaurant may be both their dining room and clubhouse. It is also the place where the people of Hong Kong celebrate domestic events and public festivals, so it is here that the visitor, with all too little time to make friendships in Hong Kong, can begin to become aware of the common bonds and the environmental differences that lie between East and West.

*The ubiquitous dragon right, once the badge of the Imperial family, still a Chinese national symbol and, perhaps even more significantly included among the deified forces of nature in Taoism, here stands guard at the imposing entrance to a floating restaurant.*

Hong Kong at night provides an idyllic opportunity to take a romantic ride in a sampan and sample the food sold by the kitchen sampans that rove about the bay dispensing snacks and cooked meals.

Alternatively the tourist may visit one of the palatial floating restaurants, such as the Tai Pak or the Jumbo on these pages, at Aberdeen, Hong Kong Island. This is the domain of the Boat People or Tanka, who are often willing to earn a little extra money by ferrying people to and fro.

On the south side of Hong Kong Island, in the old protected harbor of Aberdeen *above left, below and right, modern housing projects overlook a floating village.*

Above: *the passing out parade at the modern training school for the Royal Hong Kong Police.*

Part of the mystery of Hong Kong cuisine... left, *squid are hung up to dry in the gentle sea breezes.*

Hong Kong's coastline is a string of golden beaches, washed by crystal clear, sheltered waters such as those below. Shek O left is a particularly popular resort for sun-worshippers So too, is the palm-fringed Repulse Bay above and right, overlooked by the gracious old Repulse Bay Hotel, a last vestige of colonial days.

# Opium and Silver

THE history of Hong Kong as a trading center is a tale accompanied by the heady smell of opium and the tinkle of silver. At first, traders eager to forge commercial links with China introduced the drug illegally to those with whom they sought to do business; today, the descendants of those same traders are anxious about the high rate of drug addiction in their community.

The story began in the sixteenth century when the Portuguese founded Macao to the southwest of present-day Hong Kong. For two hundred years this port was a trading center and a missionary outpost, but as other nations moved in to compete for the China tea trade, the bulk of commercial activity moved up the Pearl River to Canton. Among the newcomers to China were Americans, Dutch and above all British, whose dominance of the seas soon made them the most important commercial power in the East.

The unquenchable British thirst for tea led the traders, prominent among whom were two Scotsmen, William Jardine and James Matheson, to try to open up a broader base for trade with the Chinese. They were rebuffed by the Emperor, who had no desire to allow the barbarians to mingle with his own people, and who was not interested in their products. Moreover, the Emperor demanded that the tea which the British traders sought should be paid for in silver. This one-way trading hardly suited the British, who soon discovered a useful expedient which tipped the balance of trade back their way and stopped the drain on their silver: they began bringing to China the opium which grew abundantly in India and charging the Chinese in silver for it. This trade, though carried on discreetly, was not actually illegal and involved the Chinese authorities along the coast as much as it did the shippers. By 1837, the opium imported into China amounted to over 40,000 cases a year and was worth millions of pounds.

At this point the Emperor of China, aware of the drug's effects on his people and of its drain on the country's silver resources, decided to make the trade illegal. He sent General Lin Tse-hsu, an opium-hater who had eliminated the smoking of the drug in Hu-Kuang, to Canton with instructions that he should stamp out the drug business.

General Lin, an energetic and dedicated man, immediately demanded that all opium should be surrendered, and made death by strangulation the punishment for anyone who disobeyed the new rule. He ordered the Hong merchants, who acted as entrepreneurs in the opium business, to persuade the British to obey his orders. Since the Canton warehouses were bulging with opium chests which represented a considerable investment for the traders, every effort was made to appear to acquiesce without actually doing so. General Lin was offered a thousand cases of opium as a gesture of appeasement but, being a man of principle, he refused this bribe and ordered his troops to besiege the warehouses. The British had no alternative but to surrender their opium, and Captain Elliot, the Superintendent of Trade, handed over 20,000 cases.

Intoxicated by his success, General Lin now followed up by ordering all the British traders to sign personal bonds of life and death before bringing their ships in to Whampoa. Captain Elliot refused and transferred all the British people from Canton to Macao. While they were there, an incident in Kowloon moved the impending showdown towards crisis point. A Chinese fisherman was killed in a brawl involving British sailors and General Lin demanded that a seaman should be handed over for punishment. Elliot refused and General Lin retaliated by ordering that the British in Macao should be left without servants or food. Wishing to remain neutral, the Portuguese fell in with the General's request and once again Elliot was obliged to evacuate the British families, this time to ships in Hong Kong harbor.

While the British were awaiting further developments, General Lin threatened to destroy the British merchant fleet. This time he had gone too far and Elliot, with two frigates, attacked the Chinese ships that had arrived in the Pearl River estuary and sank four of them, damaging most of the rest.

While this was going on, China traders in London, led by Jardine and Matheson, were trying to stir the British Government into action by persuading Palmerston, the Foreign Secretary, that the only solution to the ill-treatment of British families in China was war. In February 1840, Palmerston ordered an expeditionary force to sail from India to China.

The Opium Wars of 1840 and 1841, as they came to be called, were short and provide a copybook example of gunboat diplomacy. Four thousand troops in 16 warships with 31 supporting vessels arrived in Hong Kong and advanced up the coast to the very gateway to Peking. The Emperor, persuaded by this show of force, promised the British that they could return to Canton but promptly changed his mind. After fighting at Nanking, where the Imperial troops were defeated, the British gained the concessions that they had sought. Five trading ports were opened up and Hong Kong Island became a British possession.

By this time, the opium trade had already been renewed and continued unabated until 1907 when China and Britain agreed to end it. Smoking opium did not finally become illegal until 1946.

*Festival lanterns are the delight of bright-eyed children who carry them through the streets right. In addition to these more conventional shapes, the paper lanterns come in many forms with varying symbolic associations, such as butterflies for longevity or lobsters for mirth.*

The Chinese Opera is the most popular surviving theatrical tradition, in which ancient stories are conveyed with elaborate headdresses and stylized gestures, laden with symbolism.

Displayed in the street markets are the clothing, toys and small appliances *above, below and right, with which the Colony has flooded the globe, to become one of the world's top exporting nations.*

*Oblivious to the surrounding flurry of activity, an artist* above left *works serenely on a portrait and a fortune teller* left *stands by as a carefully trained bird selects someone's future with its beak.*

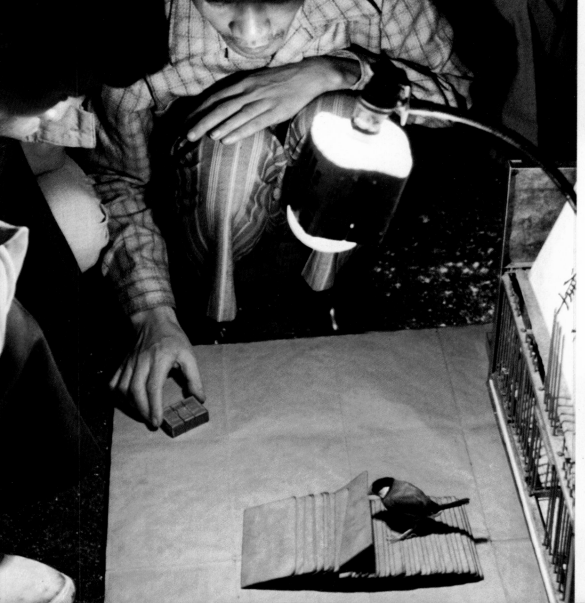

Something like 3,000 restaurants compete with each other in Hong Kong to produce the most superb cuisine. A vast range of ingredients, prepared with meticulous care and spiced with a sprinkling of philosophy result in culinary masterpieces, intended not only to tickle the palate but also to promote health and thereby bring harmony to life.

The exoticism of the food is often not matched by the decor. Local residents require simply a room in which to eat and tables are frequently large as below, to accommodate family parties.

The morning mist hangs heavily over sultry Hong Kong overleaf.

*Despite a proliferation of new highways and flyover systems, Hong Kong's multitude of cars, trams and buses below left and below are a constant cause of traffic jams. It was in an attempt to resolve an increasingly difficult traffic situation that the Mass Transit Railway right was constructed and the initial system is still in the process of expansion. Its air-conditioned stations, tunnels and trains belong, like the funicular railway above and above right and the hydrofoil below right, to the trend of modern development but in the process of innovation the traditional is not altogether lost. The Chinese junk above left still has basically the same hull shape as the Santa Maria used by Christopher Columbus.*

# 'Made In Hong Kong'

EVERYONE knows about those smart men's suits and women's dresses that Hong Kong tailors can make up in 24 hours, about the tax-free jewelry, watches, radios and televisions sets, and the vast array of goods from silk shirts and mechanical toys to Christmas tree decorations that, with their 'Made in Hong Kong' or 'Empire-made' labels, find their way to so many countries in the Western world. But perhaps very few people realize how recent the Hong Kong miracle has been.

When Captain Charles Elliot RN accepted the island of Hong Kong from the Chinese as part of Britain's compensation following the Opium Wars in 1841, he thought that he had done the correct thing to safeguard British future trading interests on the China coast. Neither Queen Victoria nor Viscount Palmerston, her Foreign Secretary, agreed; Palmerston went so far as to say that all he gained was a bare rock which could never become a Mart of Trade.

The Queen and Foreign Secretary were, of course, both wrong, though it was well over a century before they were proved so. Hong Kong has become one of the major trading centers of the Far East today, but it has not been an easy transition. In the nineteenth and early twentieth centuries, as long as Britain remained a major sea and trading power in the world, Hong Kong's role was that of an outpost guarding the sea routes and providing a haven for the ships that sailed the seven seas under the sign of the Red Duster. Warehouses, banking houses and docks sprang up and the Colony, with its population of about a quarter of a million Chinese and a handful of British residents, prospered.

In the period between the two World Wars, Britain's waning power and the militancy of mainland China made things difficult for the Colony and World War II almost brought about its eclipse. There now occurred one of those unpredictable combinations of circumstances which can totally change the destiny of nations. Vast numbers of refugees began to arrive in Hong Kong from the mainland following the Communist revolution in the late 1940s; by 1962 over three million of them had made their homes in the Colony and were looking for work. At the same time, this was a period of business expansion throughout the Western world. With these two propitious conditions, confidence in the future of the Colony began to be restored.

Today Hong Kong has a population of four and a half million and its revenue has risen from under two thousand million in the 1960s to nearly seven and a half thousand million Hong Kong dollars today. In the midst of all this business activity stand the Hong Kong and Shanghai Bank and the Bank of China. The presence of the latter is both a reassurance and a threat to the Hong Kong business world. For the Chinese, Hong Kong has long been a major source of foreign exhange and a gateway for trade with the West. The benefits that China derives depend on the success of the Colony as a business center: it seems reasonable to suppose, therefore, that the People's Republic would wish such a situation to continue. On the other hand it must be borne in mind that an old-time imperialist colony on Chinese soil must provoke some ideological heart-searching for the Communists. Under the shadow of this enigma the inhabitants, most of them Chinese, though nominally British if born in Hong Kong, carry on working and contributing to the wealth of the Colony.

The main domestic products exported are textiles and ready-made clothing, plastics and electrical goods. There is no heavy industry but increasing competition from other Asian countries, such as Korea and Singapore, has led to an intensive drive to increase the production of precision instruments which already represent a sizable percentage of the export market.

Not all of Hong Kong's workers are in modern factories or industrial plants; much of the Colony's exports and many of the pretty knick-knacks bought by tourists come from so-called cottage industries. There are also the dressmakers who can produce a copy of a dress featured in a fashion magazine at short notice, or the tailors and shirt makers who can do the same for men. Small jewelers' workshops turn out exquisite rings and necklaces, and furniture makers and artists can produce exact copies of classical Chinese works of art.

Many of these people work in conditions which, to a Westerner, are reminiscent of the sweat shops of nineteenth-century industrial Europe and Britain. Be that as it may, the work thus made available enables the workers to maintain a standard of life which is well above that of their equals in other countries. It is all a question of supply and demand and in pragmatic Hong Kong this is the rule of business life.

With a late awareness of the value of its work force, Hong Kong has set about improving living standards and thereby ensuring its cooperation in the common task of keeping the Colony one jump ahead of its rivals. New housing estates have been built to provide workers with something better than the shanty towns they have endured in the past. Full medical facilities have been made available to all, and social welfare provides programs of community services, social rehabilitation courses and help for the elderly. Public assistance is given and the government plans to make free compulsory education available to all children.

Until now the strange partnership of a Chinese work force made up largely of mainland refugees, and British administration backed by Western know-how and capital, has succeeded quite dramatically; the future may well depend as much on the successful evolution of this partnership as on external events.

*The wide brimmed straw hat trimmed with its dark valence identifies this woman left, her face prematurely aged by hard physical labor, as belonging to the Hakka, descendants of a race of wanderers who came from North China centuries ago.*

*Overleaf: The sun rises over the vast checkerboard of the fresh water fish ponds in the New Territories.*

Beyond the human turmoil of Kowloon stretch the patchwork green of paddyfields, the vitreous sheen of duck ponds and the undisturbed expanse of the New Territories,these pages and overleaf. Leased from China for 99 years, the mountains and valleys of the New Territories are the home of fishermen and farmers, who have lived in the area for hundreds of years.

Farming in Hong Kong means primarily the raising of pigs, chickens and ducks, and the cultivation of vegetables, above all rice, the mainstay of the Chinese diet. Rice seedlings are cultivated in nurseries for forty days and then transplanted to paddies where they are harvested after sixty to seventy days to produce some of the half million tons consumed in the colony each year.

Below: *A Royal Hong Kong Police Officer befriends village children.*

First published in Great Britain 1979 by Colour Library International Ltd.
© Illustrations: Colour Library International Ltd.
Colour separations by Fercrom, Barcelona, Spain.
Display and text filmsetting by Focus Photoset, London, England.
Printed and bound by Rieusset, Barcelona, Spain.
ISBN 0-8317-4541-X Library of Congress Catalogue Card No. 79-2061
**Published in the United States of America by Mayflower Books, Inc., New York City**
**Published in Canada by Wm. Collins and Sons, Toronto**